8/19

5 - SEP 2019

D0297358

*Clean Your Home
and Raise Your Spirits!*

The Secret Cleaner is a busy mum of two,
originally from America, now living on
the west coast of Scotland. She is a self-
confessed rage cleaner turned cleaning
enthusiast. She transformed the way
she thinks about cleaning, and wants to
change your mind about cleaning too.
This is the realist's, minimalist's guide to
cleaning – efficient, no-nonsense methods,
grounded in science.

The Little Book
of
Cleanfulness

The Secret Cleaner

POP PRESS

Contents

Introduction:
What is Cleanfulness?

There's a revolution happening, and it's all about cleaning! I'm here to explain why you should sit up and pay attention.

Cleaning *is* the new Zen.

You might be asking yourself what cleaning has to do with meditation, as it might not leave you feeling very calm. But keep reading …

This book is not about turning you into a domestic god or goddess, or becoming a slave to bleach. It is about making your peace with cleaning.

We all lead busy lives, so we need time-friendly but effective ways to stay on top of the daily, weekly and monthly chores that can pile up and make us feel defeated.

Being mindful is a well-known therapy for stress, anxiety, depression and low mood. In a time of change in my own life, I discovered that I could use mindfulness while cleaning – or 'cleanfulness', as I now call it – to improve my mood and my physical environment at the same time. I want to share my learning with you.

In this book, you will find simple, tried-and-tested ideas to help you keep your home – and life – in order. Nothing fancy, nothing time-consuming … just quick steps to get you on the path to a more harmonious home life.

You don't have to use them all. Pick those that work best for you and your lifestyle. Dip in and out of the book. If you are feeling overwhelmed with a million tasks, open this book and choose one thing to do.

Check Your Mood

The first thing I want you to do is to ask
yourself how cleaning makes you feel.
I don't mean how having a clean house
makes you feel – I haven't met anyone yet
who thinks that having a clean and tidy
home is depressing! But how does having
to clean make you feel? Does the relentless
list of chores leave you feeling anxious,
confused and angry? Are you overwhelmed
at the thought of tidying and cleaning?

Cleaning is a task we all must do – unless you have a team of helpers who clean your loo and pick your clothes off your floor for you. In which case, lucky you – why are you reading this book?! So many of us find cleaning and tidying tedious and even stressful. We put it off for as long as possible – which, by the way, just makes it worse.

Cleaning really doesn't need to be your enemy. By the end of this book, I want you to have changed your relationship with cleaning. I want you to have learned how to think about cleaning as a solution, rather than a cause of stress and worry. I know how crazy that sounds, but bear with me.

The amazing thing about humans is that we can change the way we think about things. An annoyance, like cleaning, can be turned into a challenge or discovery, if you just adjust the way you see it.

By reframing the way you think about cleaning, you can become less stressed, more confident – and even grow to enjoy it!

The Rage Clean

Are you a rage cleaner?

A few years ago, I noticed a pattern in my mood when I tidied and cleaned. I was always angry, annoyed and short-tempered. I flew around the house shouting at my husband, Peter, and our children, whipping everyone into a frenzy of negative emotions as I went.

When I sat down and really thought about it, I recalled my childhood. I always had a messy room back then, and I remember being in trouble for it quite a lot. I wonder if my brain held on to the link between feelings of anger, shame and frustration and tidying or cleaning for decades.

The link worked both ways – if I was angry, I would clean; and if I was cleaning, I became angry. I identified this pattern, and I recognised the cycle I was in. If I let it continue, my children would probably end up the same way, and then their children would, and so on until the end of time.

Or I could stop it.

So I decided to change my mind about cleaning. I decided to make it fun and enjoyable. My son and daughter now have more positive experiences of looking after their home, and we are building on those experiences every day. We share household chores between the four of us, and this is another key part of our approach to maintaining a happier house.

Becoming aware of this was a game changer for me. The next time you are tidying or cleaning your home, take a moment to check on your mood:

- How are you feeling about what you're doing?

- What thoughts are going through your mind?

- How are the other people in your home feeling about you doing this work?

Angry?

Resentful?

Frustrated?

Exhausted?

Cross?

Rushed?

You are not alone.

Redirecting the Rage Clean

So you're looking at a mess. Getting cross about it isn't going to help anyone. Before you start clearing it up, decide to accept the task at hand.

There's a job to do. You can choose to let it ruin your mood and everyone else's, or you can choose to tackle it and then move on with your day.

Look at the following list and find the section that most applies to how you feel and/or how you'd like to feel, and try some of the ideas it contains:

Do a HIIT clean

Set a timer on your phone – 15, 30 minutes, whatever you've got. Clean as hard as you can, then stop when the timer goes off. Admire your handiwork and move on with your day. If you have 30 minutes to spend, you could spend all 30 minutes in one room or you could do 10 minutes in three different rooms. You'll be amazed by how much you can get done in a short, fixed amount of time.

Dive in

Where to start? Look around the room and choose the first place you see that looks like it needs attention. Deal with it. Don't overthink it, just do it. Doing something is always better than doing nothing. Remind yourself that you will feel so much better for it.

Offer yourself a reward

When you've achieved what you set out to do, watch your favourite TV programme, make a cup of tea, go for a walk … Rewarding yourself with small treats is a great way to make the emotions linked to cleaning and tidying more positive.

Resentful to Thankful

Delegate it

Assign tasks to everyone in the family and give them a time limit. At the end, let them inspect each other's work. Focus on the positive. Point out the parts they did well and take the opportunity to teach them how to improve on the areas they haven't mastered yet.

Find a cleaning buddy

Do you know a friend or family member
who could help motivate you? Ask
them to hold you accountable – just like
a fitness buddy would, only for tasks
around the home.

Talk it out

Try putting a friend on speakerphone and doing your cleaning together while you chat. You will be so busy chatting, you won't even notice how much you've worked.

Make it child's play

I will never forget my son's first
childminder. She always incorporated
learning into her daily routine – using
moments like doing laundry together to
learn numbers, colours and much more.
One of my favourite things to do with the
kids when they were little was a game I call
'Laundry Avalanche'. They still love it. Get
them to lie on the floor or bed and pour
all of the clean washing over them. Make
laundry angels, roll around in it, bury them
in it, then sit together and fold it.

Frustrated to Relieved

Embrace the mess

Accept that your home is lived in and will never be perfect. If your kid is playing with toys, leave them alone. You can tidy any mess up together later.

Problem-solve

Come up with practical solutions to your
challenges. When my daughter was little,
she was terrible about leaving apple cores
in the living room. The closest bin was in
the bathroom. I bought a special bin for the
living room and tucked it next to the sofa.
She never left an apple core out again.

Do a before and after

Take a photo of a job you need to tackle.
Get stuck in and then take a picture of the
result. Share it with others or keep it to
yourself, but take a moment to bask in your
success. If you want a place where you can
document your journey to a cleaner, tidier
home, consider getting your own social
media account – you don't have to use
your real name. Believe it or not, there will
be people all over the world interested in
seeing your progress.

Confused to Clear

Crowdsource it

Stained mattress? Water marks on the wooden table? Dusty blinds? You can bet that someone has already come across this problem and solved it. Look it up on the internet, or post a question on social media or in a chat forum. Get excited about experimenting with the suggestions you get.

Try something new

The next time you need to stock up, head to the cleaning aisle of your favourite shop and have a look. REALLY have a look. Don't just reach for the same stuff you always buy – see if there's something new you can try.

Interested in making your own, more natural, eco-friendly, cruelty-free products? Have a look and see if any of the recipes at the back of this book (see pp. 106–116) catch your eye.

Demotivated to Motivated

Watch someone else clean

There are hundreds – if not thousands – of YouTube channels, vlogs and social media accounts dedicated to cleaning and organising. I defy anyone to watch a video of someone cleaning and not be motivated to get up and do something in their own home. Just make sure you don't compare your home to anyone else's, and remember that vloggers are only showing you what they want you to see.

Do some research

If you are like me, you need to know
how things work. Why does bleach kill
norovirus? What's the difference between
biological and non-biological detergents?
How does bicarbonate of soda absorb
odour? Do some research, so you can be a
more informed consumer.

Ask for advice

People love being asked to share the way they do things. Asking someone for tips can be a great conversation starter: 'How do you stay on top of your housework and work full-time?' Or more specific questions, such as – 'What do you use to clean your fridge?'

This is an especially good conversation to have with a parent or grandparent, as they are usually only too happy to share their cleaning know-how.

Set yourself a challenge
- or challenge a friend

There's nothing like a good bit of
competition to spur you on to success.

Fake it 'til you make it

Cleaning can feel like another layer of
unwanted pressure if we let it. So make a
conscious decision not to think about it
in that way.

Focus on your task and tell yourself that
you are doing something interesting and
worthwhile, even if you don't feel that
way quite yet.

Going Minimal

If you don't want a product or never use it, let it go. I used to keep a bottle of daily shower spray in my shower. I didn't like the strange fruity smell, I didn't really rate it as a cleaner and I never used it. But it sat there in my shower tray for months before I finally decided to get rid of it.

The 10 things you need

Most cleaning tasks can be tackled extremely well with a few basic products, and they are probably things you already have in the house. Don't rush out and buy anything else – get started now with what you have already, such as:

1. **Water**. The best natural cleaner there is. Sometimes just hot water will do the trick.

2. **Washing-up liquid**. Designed specifically for removing grease and food, and always worth a try.

3. **Biological washing powder or liquid**. Full of enzymes to get rid of stains. Great when used diluted on fabrics.

4. **White vinegar**. An acid that cuts through build-up such as soap scum and limescale.

5. **Lemon juice**. Another acid, but this one has a lovely smell.

6. **Bicarbonate of soda**. An alkali that is great at cutting through grease and removing odours.

7. **Scourers**. Modern or old-fashioned steel wool will break up stubborn deposits.

8. **Cleaning cloths**. Microfibre cloths have millions of tiny fibres to grab and remove microscopic dirt and bacteria. Old-fashioned cotton or muslin cloths are also very effective.

9. **Bleach**. Kills viruses, bacteria and fungi, and gets rid of stains.

10. **Gloves**. Protect your hands from heat and chemicals, and help keep them soft.

Most people have way more cleaning products and organisational clobber than they actually need in order to be able to clean their homes. Chances are, you have a cupboard bulging with cleaners that all do more or less the same thing. How many different sprays do you need for one kitchen, anyway?

Having just a few key products is great for so many reasons. Most products come in plastic bottles, so you are reducing the amount of plastic you consume. If we buy less, companies will produce less – and so will use less energy and fewer resources. You also save on space, and don't forget you'll be saving money!

Do a stock take

Start by gathering all your cleaning products together in one place. Check the bathroom cupboards, under the kitchen sink, in the garage – anywhere they might be lurking.

Theme your cleaning products

What's for the bathroom, the kitchen ...
what's a specialty cleaner, or for general
use? If you have several of the same type of
cleaner, think about why that might be the
case. Did you buy a new one because the
old one wasn't very good, but decided to
keep the old one anyway? Did you forget
you already had one and bought another?
Maybe you fell victim to a too-good-to-
pass-up offer in the shop? You need to be
honest with yourself.

You can stocktake with anything in the
home. Decide what you want to look at –
whether it's towels, pens or glasses. Go
around the house and gather everything in

this category. Lay it all out and look at what you have. Sometimes seeing it all in one place really makes you think. ('Do I really need nine duvet covers?') This is a great first step on your journey to less.

Ask yourself how many is reasonable. For example, the rule in my house is two duvet covers per bed, so we have six in our house. Once you decide, don't go back on it. Practise the rule of one in, one out. If you decide that you need ten mugs in your home, but you see one you love or someone gives you one as a gift, you now need to decide which one needs to go. Start the habit of doing this when you walk into the house with a new purchase – don't wait until later.

Consolidate any partly used duplicates

Make sure you only do this with identical products, because mixing chemicals – even if they are similar – can be deadly. Definitely not the kind of clean bomb you want! Most bottles and some spray nozzles can be recycled. Save a few to reuse for your own homemade cleaners (see pp. 106–116). Challenge yourself to wait to buy more until you have used up what you have.

Check use-by dates

Did you know that bleach only has a shelf life of 12 months? Diluted bleach is only good for 24 hours. Dispose of any cleaners that are out of date. Check the label on each product to see how to get rid of it safely.

Donate unwanted cleaning products

Give any unused and unwanted products to your local food bank, Women's Aid service, or friends and family.

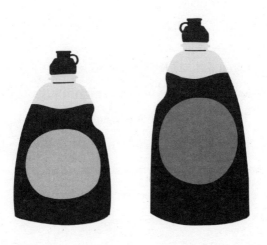

Making Cleanful Choices

Think about what is important to you in your home. How do you want it to function? What type of life do you want?

If you want a life of less dusting, aim for clear surfaces with no knick-knacks. This means that a quick once-over with a cloth or duster is all you need to put some sparkle back into your home. A mantelpiece covered in candles and vases takes a lot longer to clean.

Want to do less washing? Get into the habit of putting your clothes away and wearing them again. A quick spray of fabric refresher (see p. 115) is sometimes all you need to get another wear out of a garment.

Want to save time? Store products in the area where they are used. Keep bathroom

cleaners and cloths in your bathroom, for example, so you are not walking back and forth to get them from a central location. After you wash your cloths and sponges, make sure you spread some around the home so you can wipe the bathroom radiator the moment you notice it's dusty.

Choose to do a little every day by developing your own routine – or adopting someone else's. Saturdays might be the day you change your sheets; Sundays could be for cleaning your bathroom; and Mondays for cleaning windows. It doesn't matter how you do things – just pick a schedule that works for you and stick to it. Taking this approach breaks the tasks down into smaller chores and spreads them across the week. There will still be things that you'll need to do each day to keep on top of the housework, but this will make bigger chores seem less daunting.

I have a list of chores that get done every day in my house. Whatever happens, these are my bare minimum:

1. Wipe bathroom surfaces

2. Vacuum high-traffic areas

3. Wash and put away dishes

4. Wipe kitchen surfaces and dining table

5. Wash and put away one load of laundry

6. Make the bed

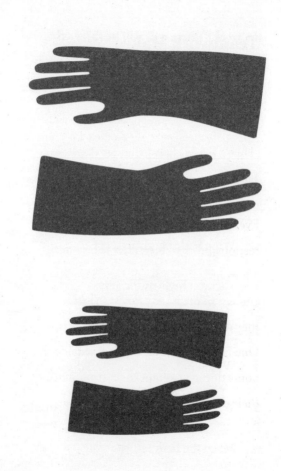

Teamwork Makes
the House Work

Everyone in the family has a
responsibility to look after their home
environment. If a small child is old
enough to drag a toy down the stairs,
they are old enough to take it back up.
One family member working outside the
home doesn't exempt them from putting
their dirty dishes in the dishwasher.

Unfair distribution of work can lead to resentment and undermine relationships. If this is a sensitive subject in your household, call a family meeting and talk about it.

If you feel like you are the one always left to do the tidying and cleaning, you might be tempted to start out by explaining how you feel, which could lead to an argument. Instead, start by asking family members how they feel about their home. Is it well looked after? How do they feel they contribute? Once you have listened to them, ask them to listen to you and let them know how you feel. Explain that you would like to come up with a system for tasks.

Propose that everyone has their own jobs, even if it's just putting their things away. You might want to think ahead about some realistic expectations for each family member.

Write up a list and place it somewhere visible. Don't forget to follow up regularly, to check everyone is doing their part. New habits take a lot longer than you think to bed in.

Don't Invite Clutter In

In today's consumer society, we are constantly informed about things we need to have. I was inspired by a woman I read about a few years ago, who went a whole year without buying anything new – apart from necessities like food, obviously. While that might be a bit extreme, it is worth thinking about how much stuff we buy that we don't need and will probably never use. I have things in my house I don't even want! Could you go a week without buying anything? A month?

Once something arrives in your home, you develop a kind of emotional connection to it, and this makes it even harder to get rid of. One challenge for me is shopping bags. I have a huge selection of reusable bags – they are so pretty and useful! When I try to pare them down (which I often do), I find it difficult because 'this one is really good for holidays' and 'this one is great for folding up into other bags'. I end up finding a reason to keep them all. It's easier to not get them in the first place.

After having my second baby, I remember sitting in the hospital with my bag of goodies from the rep who visited new mums. It contained useful things like free wipes, nappies and samples of detergent.

And not-so-useful things, like leaflets and booklets that I knew I would never read. Before I went home that day, I reduced the contents of that bag to only the things that I knew I would use, and left the rest in the bin in my hospital room.

The next time you put something in your trolley or are offered a freebie, think about whether you really need this thing. Let's face it – once it's in your home, it's much harder to let it go.

Clean in the Moment

Have you ever noticed an ability to laser-focus on the task of scrubbing last night's bolognese off your pan? That's because you are in the moment. You aren't thinking about the past or the future, you're just thinking about how you're going to get the burnt bits off the bottom of that (allegedly) non-stick pan.

Everyone knows that living in the moment is brilliant for mental health. Mindfulness is essentially the practice of directing your attention to the here and now. It's about experiencing life as it unfolds, not thinking about what has happened before or what might happen in the future.

When you need a break from the chaos of the rest of life, choose a job that you can really concentrate on. If you hate cleaning and tidying, work on reframing your thoughts about it. Think of it as a form of meditation. This works particularly well for really dirty or messy areas, where you can see the transformation immediately.

Try some of these in-the-moment cleans …

Carpet clean

Sprinkle some bicarbonate of soda or
carpet freshener across carpeted flooring.
Leave it to sit for an hour to absorb odours.
Start vacuuming it up. Engage all of your
senses in this job: What can you smell?
Can you see the lines your vacuum makes
in the carpet? Challenge yourself to make
a series of triangles in the floor like a
professional carpet cleaner.

What sounds does your vacuum make?
Does it sound healthy? If your vacuum
is struggling, you might find that giving
it a good clean makes it work much
more effectively.

Window clean

Pick one room and clean the windows in that room. Think about how being able to see better out of that window is brightening your day.

Make your own window-cleaning solution using the recipe on page 107. Spray a small amount onto the glass and wipe away with a cloth or paper towel.

The key to streak-free windows is keeping your cloth as dry as possible. One way to achieve this is to work the solution in with one cloth, and then use another to wipe it away. A tightly woven window cloth also really helps.

Drawer clean

Focus on just one drawer. Take everything out of the drawer, including any dividers or trays. Use your vacuum to get rid of dust and dirt, then wipe with a damp cloth. Cull any items that you don't use or need, and organise the remaining items into groups. Think about how you can best use the space. For example, to separate socks and pants, you can add shoeboxes. To tie together a set of special forks, use a rubber band. And to organise your make-up, use takeaway containers.

Wardrobe clean

Wardrobes are an easy place to hide things that don't have a home. Don't bite off more than you can chew by pulling everything out of your wardrobe and throwing it on your bed! Take it one step at a time, clear a shelf, organise the hanging items, line up your shoes …

One way to focus your efforts is to use the one-year rule: if you haven't worn something in one year, give it away, sell it or throw it away.

Oven-door clean

The oven is usually neglected because people think it's more difficult to clean than it actually is. Just focus on the glass on the inside of the oven. Use a slightly wet steel-wool scourer – not the impregnated kind with the pink soap, just the plain ones – dipped in bicarbonate of soda to remove built-up grease. Work on one quarter of the glass at a time, so you can really see the impact you are making.

The dumping-ground clean

Everyone has an area (or more than one!) where things start to pile up. Some people are just better at hiding it than others. Have a look around your house and find one of these areas. It might be a shelf, a corner of a room, or a cupboard where things just seem to get tossed when there is nowhere else for them to go.

Chances are, this area has been collecting things for a while, so don't put pressure on yourself to clear it all at once. Choose a section of the space – no more than a metre squared – and deal with that. Or, to tackle a big pile of stuff, try putting away five things each day for a week.

Creating Good Habits

Having a clean and tidy home is all about
habits. Positive habits – such as avoiding
overbuying, putting things away when
you are finished with them, and cleaning
as you go – will save you time and stress.
Prevention is always better than a cure.
If I develop a habit of wiping my shower
screen every time I use it, I am preventing
a more difficult job later. A dry shower
screen can't become stained with limescale
or covered in mould.

Most people know that they need better routines and habits, but just haven't found a way to put them into practice. See if the ideas on the following pages work for you.

Kitchen-cupboard habit

While your dinner is cooking, fill the sink with warm water and a few drops of washing-up liquid. Use a cloth to wipe down the fronts of your kitchen cabinets. Start at the top and work your way down. Make sure you go over ledges and the tops of drawers, around handles and over the front of the fridge and any other appliances you have in your kitchen. You might not make it all the way around the kitchen, but that's OK – you can pick up where you left off another day.

Soft-furnishings habit

To keep your sofas and chairs as dazzling
as the day you bought them, clean and turn
over the cushions regularly. Make sure you
are vacuuming under your sofa cushions,
as food and dirt on the frame of the sofa
is in contact with your seat cushions and
could be causing marks and stains. Many
modern sofas have zippable covers that
can be washed at home in the washing
machine. Do this twice a year. Be careful
to follow the instructions as adding water
or products to some sofas may remove
the fire-retardant coating. Swap your
cushions around weekly so you don't end

up with uneven wear and tear. If the arms of your sofa are prone to dirty handprints and coffee-cup rings, place a coaster or a blanket there to protect the fabric/leather.

Kitchen-worktop habit

This might seem simple to you but this is a habit that many people have not mastered. I remember being invited to an older friend's house for dinner many years ago. I watched as she got out a spray cleaner after dinner and wiped her surfaces down. I was genuinely amazed. I had always been a person who 'cleaned' the kitchen. I would have never thought to 'maintain' the kitchen. By maintaining her kitchen – i.e. giving it a wipe-down after she used it – she saved herself the job of trying to scrape off hardened food and scrub at stubborn stains, making the task of preparing the next meal so much easier.

Microwave habit

Wash the plate in your microwave at least once a week, and give the inside a wipe-down after each use so that food doesn't get a chance to dry on. Make sure you have a good look, especially at the ceiling, for splashes.

Fridge habit

Before you do your weekly shopping,
use a cloth soaked in warm water and
washing-up liquid to go over the shelves
and drawers. Never use highly perfumed
products in the fridge, as they can taint
foods (making them taste like chemicals),
and try to avoid bleach on the rubber seals
of your fridge (or washing machine) as it
can damage the rubber.

Oven habit

With regular wipe-downs, your oven can stay looking brand new for years. Make sure you check after each use for spills. Removing them straight away will be easy with a damp cloth.

Every couple of weeks, give your oven a quick once-over with a bit of steel wool. Whenever there's a spill, wipe it up as quickly as possible so it doesn't get baked in. If your oven needs a bit more of a clean until you can get into this routine, start by cleaning it a bit at a time until it is sparkling again.

Carpet habit

Vacuum high-traffic areas every day if possible. For most people, this includes the entryway, hall and living areas. Dirt and oils left on a carpet end up being pushed further into the pile, making them difficult to remove later. Stains are also more difficult to remove the longer they are left. So make sure you respond quickly to any spills on carpets. Train everyone in the house to report spillages urgently. No blame, no drama – just quick action.

Vacuum habit

To keep your vacuum performing well and smelling fresh, empty the cylinder after each use. Dirt and bacteria sitting inside it can give off a musty odour, especially if you have pets. If your vacuum is filling your house with eau-de-wet-dog, it's probably past time to give it a good clean (see page 126) and get into the habit of emptying it after every outing.

Woodwork habit

When I bought my first house, I must admit I had no idea how to look after it. Cleaning skirting boards and doors was a foreign concept to me. It does make me wonder if anyone ever did this job in my home growing up.

There are a few ways to tackle skirting boards. I've seen some people dust them with their socked feet! I suggest you deal with them during regular vacuuming so the dust doesn't build up. But if you are contending with an existing build-up, add a few drops of washing-up liquid to a bowl of warm water, and use a microfibre cloth to remove the dust.

The same applies to doors. Regular wiping with a wet cloth is usually enough to keep them dust- and dirt-free. In my experience, the more small children and animals you have, the more often you need to do this.

Make-your-bed habit

Your bed takes up a lot of floor and visual space in your bedroom. A great way to give the impression of tidiness is to simply make the bed. It doesn't have to be done to the standard of a luxury hotel. Just spread your duvet or blanket out across the bed and place the pillows at the top.

Bathroom habit

Wipe over the surfaces in your bathroom regularly. When you wash your hands, take a few seconds to wipe the sink and tap using your hands. After you have a shower, use a microfibre cloth or a squeegee to remove excess water and steam from your shower screen and bathroom mirror. Before bed, add toilet cleaner to the loo and leave it to work overnight. Always be careful to ventilate the room when using bleach.

Quick-tidy habit

Use your new cleanfulness mindset to tidy as you go. Always tidy minor messes when you see them. If something can be done in under a minute, there's no excuse not to do it there and then. Each night before bed, have a scan of your main living area and remove any items that don't belong.

Dusting habit

Dusting doesn't have to be complicated. You don't need a special tool or product to do it. I use dusting as a chance to inspect and care for the things that I have on display in my home, wiping over surfaces with a slightly damp cloth. When I'm feeling like a change, I enjoy rearranging decorative items and giving the room a whole new look.

Bins habit

When was the last time you cleaned your bins? If you leave it too long, it becomes a daunting task, but done regularly, it's a breeze. Give the outside a quick wipe-down every day, and clean the internal parts every few weeks to keep odours at bay.

A Place for Everything
and Everything in its Place

It's probably the world's biggest cleaning cliché but …

Everything. Needs. A. Place.

I was looking for the Sellotape the other day. I could think of four possible locations it could be: the box with the wrapping paper and cards; the cupboard where the home-decorating things are kept; the kitchen junk drawer; or one of the kids' rooms. You can imagine how my frustration built as I wandered around the house looking for it, shouting out, 'Has anyone seen the Sellotape?'

You might think the answer is to buy more Sellotape and keep a roll in each of those places, and that is one possible solution – but as far as I know, adding more stuff has never helped anyone in their quest to keep a tidier home.

To prevent wasted time and tested tempers caused by losing items around the house, think about where things go and make sure everyone knows. With children (and some adults), you might need to give reminders, but it'll be worth it in the end.

There are a couple of ways you can tackle this challenge:

- Keep things where you are most likely to need them. Garden shears are hardly going to be any use in the bathroom.

- Keep things with their 'families'. Wrapping paper, ribbon, tape, scissors and cards can all be stored together.

Progress NOT Perfection

Are you unhappy because your house is a mess, or is your house a mess because you are unhappy?

Your environment has a huge impact on your sense of well-being. Sitting around in a house that is disorganised and dusty can be a right downer, leading to a cycle of feeling low and stuck in a rut. But while you might not know how to fix your mood, you do know how to clean your house – so start there.

Our brains have a sneaky way of telling us that there's no point starting a big task. You don't have the right product … It'll take too long … You'll be interrupted … It's just too enormous … It'll just get dirty again … and so on! So, it never gets done.

My classic behaviour was to decide I'd need to completely reorganise a room. In order to do this, I'd need to go shopping for the perfect storage boxes. I would have an exact image of what I wanted and I'd spend the day scouring the shops for it. Many times, I would return home deflated, having not found what I was looking for. Imagine if I had spent that time doing the job instead! Think about how much I could have achieved if I had spent those hours

being productive instead of distracting
myself with a shopping trip.

Perfection is the Enemy of Progress

Don't wait to clean or tidy until you have
the right product, the perfect storage box
or a full day to spend on it. That's just your
brain's way of procrastinating on a job you
don't want to tackle. Start before you're
ready, but start small. You want to aim for
progress, not perfection. Beware of the
unattainable clean. Your house is a home,
not a feature in a magazine – it can't be
spotless all the time.

When you start with something small,
it gives you two things:

1. **Accomplishment.** OK, so you haven't cleared out the whole wardrobe, but you have cleared one shelf and that shelf looks amazing!

2. **Momentum.** Once you see how great your space begins to look, and you experience the hit of feel-good hormones associated with your achievement, you'll want to do more. An object at rest stays at rest, and an object in motion stays … in MOTION!

Pick your least favourite task – the one you've been putting off – and do that first. If it's too big to complete in the time you've got, break it down into smaller chunks.

When you take this approach, everything from that point onwards is a breeze. You'll feel successful and proud of what you've achieved, and that positivity will keep you going.

Ten small wins that make a big visual
difference to a room but don't take much
time are:

1. Make the bed

2. Plump the sofa cushions

3. Open the curtains/draw the blinds

4. Put the dishes away

5. Clean the sink

6. Vacuum

7. Shine the kettle or toaster

8. Clear the table

9. Put a load of washing on

10. Wipe the bathroom surfaces

Break a daunting job down

By doing small projects that help you associate cleaning with a feeling of achievement and pride, your brain will begin to rewire your thought pathways. Every time you experience a success, your brain will crave more of that good feeling. Need to clear the garage? Divide it into six sections and clear one section each week. Yes, that means it will take you six weeks to finish it, but how long have you been putting it off already? Clearing $\frac{1}{6}$ of a garage is better than clearing $\frac{0}{6}$ of a garage!

Do one thing at a time

Another facet of cleanfulness is steadying
the mind – reducing the background
noise of distracting thoughts and the
temptation to multitask. If you are tidying
your bedroom, and you come across a
few cups and plates, don't be tempted
to take them to the kitchen. I'm betting
there are probably other jobs there that
will draw you in. Instead, stay in the
room you are cleaning for as long as
possible. Put things away elsewhere only
when you have made so much progress
that you can't do anything else.

Tackling the out-of-control

For out-of-control rooms (usually my kids'
bedrooms), I use a thematic approach.
I clear surfaces, storage baskets, junk
drawers – EVERYTHING – and put
it all into a giant pile on the floor, to be
reorganised and then put away.

You will need:
one bag for rubbish
one bag for charity
one washing basket

Sort everything into piles with similarly
themed items, e.g. books, clothes, cuddly
toys, hair baubles …

At the end of the sorting process, have a look at the existing storage arrangements and see if these need to change or not. If there is a huge pile of cuddly toys but the only big box has been used for a few pieces of Lego, for example, then swap them around.

Be ruthless with junk

Toys that are never played with and bits of old homework will always get the heave-ho in my house. The way I see it, if your kids want the privilege of deciding what to keep and what to throw away, they need to take responsibility for cleaning their own rooms! Be careful not to get too carried away, though. I once threw away my husband's only pair of work shoes thinking they were an old pair that he didn't wear.

Get Inspired

Feeling stuck in a rut? Bored with the same old chores, day in, day out? Put some fun into your cleaning routine! Humans need variety.

One way to spice up your cleaning and tidying is to try something completely new, something that pushes you out of your comfort zone.

With the rise of the online cleaning community, one way many people are choosing to do this is by opening Instagram accounts under aliases, where they can share their cleaning experiences and tips online.

Here are a few more ideas to bring some fun back into cleaning …

Act it out

Choose a job to do, and act it out like you're on a TV cleaning programme or a YouTube video. Kids love this one. (Shh, don't tell them they're helping!)

Assign roles like director, scriptwriter, cleaner, presenter and camera person. Introduce your segment: 'Hi, everyone. Today we're going to be doing laundry! The first step is to divide your clothes into different piles …'

Go through the whole task like this. You can even choose to record it for real, and watch it back for laughs later.

Have a dance party

Use music to liven up your cleaning routine by creating a motivational cleaning playlist. Or choose three or four songs to play, and clean for the length of time they are playing – stopping when they're done.

Make a video

Most smartphones these days have a time-lapse function on the camera. This basically creates a sped-up video.

Set your phone up so that it's pointing at the job you want to do, and press record. Give yourself a time limit of 10 or 15 minutes, then stop your cleaning – and the video. Watch it back and see the transformation from when you started to when you finished. You'll be surprised how good it feels to see yourself being so productive.

For some reason, when I do this, I move a lot faster as well!

Role-play it

Imagine you are a cleaning-product tester. Grab a piece of paper and a pen, as well as a product you want to use. Inspect it carefully and read the instructions. (You'd be surprised how many people have been using products the wrong way for years!) Use it as directed, and take some notes about it ... How does it smell? Is it too foamy? Does it do a good job? Give it a star rating.

Cleanful Recipes

One way to really embrace your cleaning routine is to invest some time in developing your own arsenal of homemade cleaners. With just a few simple, natural ingredients, you can make your own products for every job in the home.

Degreaser

You need:
empty spray bottle
2 tsp washing-up liquid
125ml/½ cup white vinegar
500ml/2 cups water

Pour the water, white vinegar and washing-up liquid into the empty spray bottle. Shake well. To use, just spray on surfaces and wipe off with a sponge or cloth.

Window cleaner

You need:
empty spray bottle
250ml/1 cup white vinegar
250ml/1 cup water

Pour the water and vinegar into the spray bottle and shake. Use sparingly for cleaning windows and glass.

Dishwasher cleaner

You need:
250ml/1 cup white vinegar

You might not know that there is a filter
in the bottom of your dishwasher that can
be removed and cleaned. They can get
pretty gross with the build-up of food and
grease, so if your machine smells foul, it's
the first place to look. The bottom area
usually includes a plastic cup surrounded
by a steel plate. Both of these items can be
lifted out of the dishwasher and cleaned in
the sink with some washing-up liquid and
warm water.

For a proper clean of the rest of the machine, replace the filter and make sure there's no food in the bottom of the machine. Pour 250ml/1 cup of white vinegar into a dishwasher-safe open container and place it on the top rack of the dishwasher, then run it empty on the hottest, longest cycle.

Washing-machine cleaner

You need:
250ml/1 cup white vinegar

Remove your detergent drawer and soak it
in a sink full of soapy water to loosen any
build-up. Use a cloth or an old toothbrush
to scrub the compartment in the washing
machine where the drawer sits. Don't
forget to check the top, where mould can
sometimes begin to form. Once you've
washed the drawer thoroughly, return it
to the slot.

Use a cloth to wipe the inside of the
door and the rubber seal. Now, pour the
white vinegar into the drum of the empty
machine and set it on the hottest cycle.

When the cycle is finished, open the door and leave the machine to dry. It is a good idea to always leave your washing-machine door open after use, so that mould and mildew can't build up between washes.

Kettle descaler

You need:
half white vinegar
half water

Fill the kettle up to the half-way mark with equal parts water and white vinegar, then boil. Let the vinegar-water mix sit in the kettle for 15–20 minutes. Rinse well.

Microwave cleaner

You need:
1 lemon
125ml/½ cup water in a microwavable bowl

Cut the lemon in half and squeeze the juice
into the bowl of water. Place the lemon in
the liquid, and microwave on high for
3 minutes. Once the microwave stops, leave
it to sit for 5 minutes. Use a damp sponge
to wipe off the loosened food. You can
dip the sponge in the bowl of warm lemon
water if you need extra power. Be careful,
it might be hot.

Grout cleaner

You need:
180g/1 cup bicarbonate of soda
a few tsps water

Gradually add the water to the bicarbonate of soda until you have a thick paste. Use your hands to apply the mixture to the grout. If the consistency is right, it will stick and won't run down the tiles too much. Leave this to sit for 10 minutes then use an old toothbrush to scrub the grout, reapplying if necessary, until you are happy with the result.

Fabric refresher

You need:
empty spray bottle
250ml/1 cup warm water
1 tbsp bicarbonate of soda
essential oils (optional)

Add the bicarbonate of soda to the spray
bottle. Pour in the warm water and add
a few drops of essential oil for scent if
desired. Shake well. Suitable for use on soft
furnishings and clothing. Shake before each
use. Do not use on fire-retardant fabrics.

Carpet refresher

You need:
bicarbonate of soda

Vacuum the carpet. Sprinkle bicarb
liberally over the carpet, and leave for
as long as possible to absorb odours.
Vacuum again.

9 Things You Forgot to Clean

Once you master cleanfulness, you'll be on top of all your routine chores. Your home will be running like clockwork and you'll be ready to take on some more complicated jobs that you might not have done before. Here are a few that you might not have thought of …

Extractor filters

If you have a typical extractor filter with two little metal-mesh rectangles above your cooker, you can pop them out using a plastic button on the edge. Place them on their own in the dishwasher with a tablet only. Don't add dishwasher salt.

If you don't have a dishwasher, place them in the sink. Fill it with hot water and add a few generous squirts of washing-up liquid. You may need to repeat this process if there is a lot of grease build-up.

High-level dusting

When was the last time you looked up while you were cleaning? There are all sorts of things above eye-level: light fixtures, tops of kitchen cupboards, picture rails, ceilings … Use a long-handled duster or attach a microfibre cloth to a broom to reach high places and remove dust and cobwebs. Don't forget to dust your blinds and curtain rails.

Descale taps and shower heads

If you're in an area plagued with hard water, you'll know the struggle of keeping limescale at bay. One easy way to tackle it is to fill a plastic bag with vinegar, and use a rubber band to tie it around the shower or tap head. Leave for a few hours. Remove and then brush the head with an old toothbrush. Rinse away any deposits.

Outside doors and window frames

You've cleaned your windows, but have you looked at the window frames or inside the frames of your windows and doors? These can get incredibly dirty, especially over the winter when wind and rain drive grime into crevices. Use a cloth and your homemade window spray (see p. 107) to tackle these areas.

Inside kitchen cupboards and drawers

When was the last time you took the cutlery out of your cutlery drawer? If it's been a while, chances are there's enough food in the bottom to provide you with a decent-sized snack. (Don't eat it!) Take a minute when you can to empty a drawer or a cupboard, then vacuum out the debris and give it a wipe before putting the contents back. This is also an opportunity to get rid of any items that you haven't used recently.

Light switches, plug covers and cords

Give these a wipe with a damp cloth to remove dust and dirt build-up. Extension cords and other electric cables can get especially dirty over time. I'm sure I don't need to remind you that water and electrics aren't friends.

Radiators

Get up close and personal with your radiators. You walk past them every day, but you might not realise how dusty and tired they begin to look. A quick wipe-down will restore them to their glory. For chrome radiators, you can use your half-white vinegar, half-water solution to bring out the shine.

Behind the furniture

It seems like a big job, but it really only takes a few minutes to shift the sofa so that you can vacuum underneath. And any spare change or treasure you find is yours for the keeping!

Vacuum maintenance

Start by vacuuming, because your machine might be out of use for a day or so while your filters dry. Each machine is different, so find your user manual – or look it up online – to see how to take yours apart to clean it. Make sure your vacuum is unplugged before beginning any cleaning.

Most modern vacuums have a plastic container which can be removed and rinsed or wiped over. Sponge-like filters can be run under the tap and wrung out until the water runs clear.

Brush heads are often removable making it easier to remove hair (although not always washable – check your instructions) – but if they are not, use a small pair of scissors to remove any hair or string that has become tangled in your brush roller.

1 3 5 7 9 10 8 6 4 2

Pop Press, an imprint of Ebury Publishing,
20 Vauxhall Bridge Road,
London, SW1V 2SA

Pop Press is part of the Penguin Random House group of companies
whose addresses can be found at global.penguinrandomhouse.com

Penguin
Random House
UK

Text © The Secret Cleaner 2019
Illustrations by Fuchsia MacAree © Pop Press 2019
Design by seagulls.net

The Secret Cleaner has asserted her right to be identified as the author of this
Work in accordance with the Copyright, Designs and Patents Act 1988

First published by Pop Press in 2019

www.penguin.co.uk

A CIP catalogue record for this book is available from the British Library

ISBN: 978-1-5291-0562-9

Printed and bound in Great Britain by Clays Ltd, Elcograf S.p.A.

Penguin Random House is committed to a sustainable future for
our business, our readers and our planet. This book is made from
Forest Stewardship Council® certified paper.